Genie of the Chesapeake

Ralph Boldyga

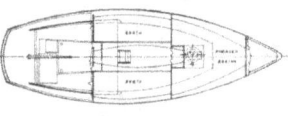

Hull Type:	Long Keel
Rigging Type:	Masthead Sloop
LOA:	23.00 ft / 7.01 m
LWL:	17.50 ft / 5.33 m
S.A. (reported):	246.00 ft² / 22.85 m²
Beam:	7.25 ft / 2.21 m
Displacement:	3,750.00 lbs. / 1,701 kg
Ballast:	1,475.00 lbs. / 669 kg
Max Draft:	2.83 ft / 0.86 m
Construction:	FG
First Built:	1965
# Built:	250
Builder:	South Coast Seacraft Co. (USA)
Designer:	Carl Alberg
S.A. / Displ.:	16.35
Bal. / Displ.:	39.33
Disp. / Len:	312.37
Comfort Ratio:	21.61
Capsize Screening Formula:	1.87
S#:	1.61
Hull Speed:	5.61 kn
Pounds/Inch Immersion:	453.34 pounds/inch

Dedication

This book is dedicated to:

Michael Thomas Strandquist, 1957 - 2016

Acknowledgments

To my loving wife of forty-four years, Terri Boldyga, for her support and understanding. For the numerous trips she made delivering meals and checking on my well-being. It's not always easy being the spouse of a Merchant Marine Captain. We know that Marine Captains are always right, misinformed perhaps, sloppy at times, fickle, bullheaded, and even stupid daredevils, but never wrong.

To my son, Brandon Boldyga, for his willingness to sail with his dad that one unforgettable day back in April of 2002. I only wish that we had sailed together more often.

To Mike Strandquist, for his words of wisdom, encouraging smiles, and helping hands. RIP, buddy.

Table of Contents

Foreword

Thank you for joining me as I share with you the story of *Genie*, the 1965 South Coast 23' sailboat and how she inspired me to become a US Coast Guard Merchant Marine Captain.

We begin this story in one of Anne Arundel County's grand marinas, in the derelict boat section that I refer to as the boneyard, where the old, weathered, neglected boats go to wait for their destruction.

It is my hope that this book inspires you to give one of those old boats that still has life in her a second look before her destruction, possibly preserving her for future generations. I would also like to encourage each of you to sail the Chesapeake and enjoy all she has to offer. If you find her brackish waters run within your veins, as it does mine, I encourage you to work her waters and obtain your Coast Guard credentials.

Now, get comfortable in your favorite reading place and join me as I share with you the story of *Genie* and her grand expedition to witness the start of leg seven, 2002 Volvo World Cup Races, Baltimore/Annapolis—La Rochelle, France. It's a story of hard work and commitment, pleasure sailing and survival sailing. This book is also a story of good folks who work the marinas along the bay's western shores and the Captain Clowns that travers her waters.

Sailed Her

Upon the planks, we walk over water to board her.
Her beautiful reflection bounces upon the ripples, where she
lies in wait.
She appears lean and fit, yearning to be rid of all constraints.
Her mast is empty, and her halyards clang as she is boarded,
Greeting each with a welcome chime.

She offers a place of refuge within her frame.

Her rigging is strong and gleaming.
A captain confident in abilities is now upon her.
She willingly yields control to her master once again.

As her lanyards are released from the pilings, she slips from
her berth.
East into the rising sun, she is guided toward the starting
line.
She greets each wave upon her bow with an upward rising,
Following a smooth glide into the trough.

Each rise and fall is taken with pleasure in a steady pulsating
beat,
Leaving only a slight wake as she passes its crest.
A fine mist is cast off of her bow as she glides toward the
starting line.
There, the colors of the rainbow are now revealed as the
rising sun is split by the prisms.

Upon her mast, great sheets have been stretched, to catch the
breath of God.
They bellow as the energy that has traversed the world is
brought upon them.
Lines drawn around the winches and strung tight through the
blocks,
The crew wrestles to bring her into compliance with the
sound of the one-minute warning.

As the crack of the gun breaks the silence, signaling the start,
She heels to the forces brought upon her as the race begins.

Continuously seeking the breath of clean air as she moves
toward the windward mark,
The rising and falling growing ever faster as she proceeds.

She points as far into the wind as she can without a luff or
hesitation,
Navigating to the first buoy with as few tacks as possible.
Her crew agleam as they round the first mark without a
touch,
A jibe, bearing way onto a downwind leg.

The sharp eye of her captain spies the second marker,
And with his firm grip at the helm, he reckons her course.
She responds to his wishes as her boom swings over the
crew.
She strains to accelerate once again as the pounding
intensifies.

Forward, she races as the bows of her challengers give chase
to her stern,
Her dinghy crew suspended horizontally over the waters,
hooked in her trapeze.
Preparing to jibe rings out, anticipating the second marker,
And with no further warning, jibe ho!

Like a flower blooming, her spinnaker is hoisted by the
strong crew,
Bellowing in an explosion of colors.
Grabbing all the air that comes her way,
She pulls herself toward the leeward mark, striving to be
first.

With subtle rolling from starboard to port, she maintains her bearing,
Tackling wave after wave as she is guided by experienced hands.
She passes the mark with the crew bursting into cheers as the air horn sounds.
The captain knows she has completed the course,
For the crew sailed her, and won!

PART I:
The Boneyard

In just about every boatyard that exists on the Chesapeake Bay, and maybe even throughout the United States, there is that section of the yard that holds the boats whose owners have lost their luster to sail or have come upon hard times and can no longer justify the resources required to maintain them.

I have walked many a boneyard in my day and spent many an hour pondering the plight of these derelict boats. You can still see the grandeur in their lines and can imagine the delight that they had once brought to their original masters. The larger the boat, the more dreadful the appearance in the forgotten section of the marina.

Many meet their fate at the loss of their captains, for it is normal that not everyone will share the bond necessary to commit one's life to maintenance. When her captain moves on to the next world, he cannot take his love with him, so their souls are separated and that of the boat's is left rotting in the boneyard. Eventually, the names are lost in the memories of time, no longer passing the lips of those who shared a ride upon their decks. Forgotten are the joys that were long ago captured in the photos of her crew as they sought clean air to fill her sails.

Other times, the boats are left due to people moving to locations where they don't have open water access, or they are left behind with thoughts of an aqueous retreat that is seldom or never used. But no matter what the chain of events that leave these boats stranded, they all have one thing in common—they are no longer loved, and the boatyards want them gone.

As these crafts fall into disrepair and their accounts become delinquent, the marinas move the lost souls to some back section of the yard where the tides cause the ground to be soft and overgrown with weeds. The area is usually one that floods, and the ground is typically not firm enough for heavy use. In the back, out of sight, this is where you find the forgotten lost souls of the boat boneyard.

Before the yard can sell or dispose of these deprived boats, they usually file liens against the titles for non-payment of storage and service fees. This is when you want to buy one of these souls, if you are interested and the opportunity presents itself. Typically, the yard will sell them for a couple hundred dollars, and sometimes you can talk the yard into selling them for just enough to cover the cost of the paperwork. The deal is you have to make a commitment to buy the services from venders that operate at the yard and, most importantly, pay for the storage and keep your account current.

When in search of a deal, I usually start by taking a drive through the rows of derelict boats, looking for signs that the owner has tried to sell her, thinking she might still be in decent shape if she was just recently assigned to this section of the marina. More often than not, she has suffered years of neglect and has passed the point of no return, as most owners stop maintaining their boats long before they let their yard fees go into arrears.

It's always best to go to the marina office and ask if there are any boats in the yard that the marina is looking to sell or if they are aware of a circumstance where the owners are looking to dispose of the boat. You never know when someone will pass away or get divorced, when they will lose a job or move to keep employment.

I am always amazed how the owners value their boat's worth to be so great. I have seen owners hold out and refuse to sell for five hundred dollars just to find the same boat in the boneyard, owned by the marina the following year due to non-payment of yard rental fees. Unfortunately, you should only own one of these boats at a time, no matter how much you want to save them all. Otherwise, you, too, risk being the one having to forfeit due to non-payment.

Too many projects at one time are a big no-no. We all know that a boat is a hole in the water to throw your money into and the two happiest days in every boat owner's life are the day you buy your boat and the day you sell her. If you can't afford the time or money to launch her and enjoy her, those two days will blend with nothing but regrets in-between.

Chapter One:
On the Hard

It was a hot summer day in July of 2001, and my wife was working at the local marina in Deale, Maryland. I found it fun to visit her at her work, being she had to do a weekend shift every Saturday. It gave us a few moments together, and I enjoyed seeing her in action. Sometimes, I would bring her lunch, flowers, or ice cream just to put a smile on her face.

Having been raised in Annapolis and an avid sailor who grew up racing out of the Severn Sailing Association (SSA), located on Fleet Street in Eastport, I never passed up the opportunity to stroll through the boatyards, admiring the boats and talking with those who sailed them. This was the highlight of my week when my honey-do list was under control.

Our oldest child had grown up and moved on with her life, and the youngest was now in his mid-teens. He did not need me hanging out with him all day, and he never really liked boating much, so the boatyard was not a real attraction to him.

While visiting the marina on this particular day, the marina manager was walking along the parking lot with a list in his hands. He was a big man, heavy set, and did not tolerate the heat well. You could tell he was doing something out in the sun that he would rather not be doing.

As I passed him by, he jokingly asked if I wanted to buy all the boats on the list so he would not have to move them. Not understanding what he meant, I questioned him further and found out that he had been asked by the marina owner to collect the bones and move them to the boneyard. Apparently, the marina had just gone through the process of placing liens on the delinquent boats for ownership. His job was now to find the boats with delinquent accounts that were scattered around the yard and get the yard crew to move them. This is always best done during the summer when the number of boats on the hard are at minimum. It is much easier to locate the boats and move them around without risking damage while there is room to maneuver.

Most of the boats that were to be used that summer had been launched by the first of July. Those that remained on the hard were either those needing repairs or those that were just unloved and on their path to dismay.

With not much to do that day, I asked if I could look at the list and tag along. He warned me that the larger the boat on the list, the more costly the rental fees would be and the greater the cost to repair. He suggested, if I was serious, that I should stick with a boat between twenty and twenty-five feet. Twenty-seven feet max was his last comment.

With that, I took his comments as an invitation to join him on his venture.

As he worked through the list, he was able to tell me the story of each boat—how long it had been sitting, if it was salvageable, who had owned it, and why their account was delinquent.

Most of the boats on his list were in total disrepair. The decks had gone soft, the scuppers had clogged and flooded the interiors, and they were basically pools on stilts. Some of the boats actually had trees growing through them and holes larger than bowling balls.

He continued his paces through the list, calling the yard crew to move each of the derelict boats to the boneyard.

Then, as we approached the boneyard section of the marina, he glanced up from his paper, squinted in the bright sunlight, and pointed to a small sailboat. "This one is salvageable," he said. She was just recently acquired.

He invited me to board her. Then he told me that the marina now owned her, and she was dry inside. I took him up on the invitation, scaling the small ladder that was erected by her side.

As I stood up on her deck, I could see she was the perfect size. Her decks were firm, her teak was intact, and she had sails. She was large enough to handle the bay on a breezy day and small enough to navigate singlehandedly.

I did have some concerns, being she was a full keel boat and did not have much freeboard. That meant she could handle the heavy winds but not necessarily choppy seas. The cost of an engine would also become an added expense that I was not necessarily ready to commit to at this point in my life, but I had an old British Seagull that just might work.

The marina manager had moved on with his task, leaving me on the deck of the sailboat. As he exited the boneyard, he shaded his eyes as he gazed back at me inspecting the craft. I could see a slight smile on his face. He then called out to me to visit the office if I was interested.

I spent the good part of an hour out there, sitting on that dirty, derelict boat. I opened her cabin, and she had all the things that every boat in the boneyard had—can after can of cleaners, fillers, caulks, glues, nuts, bolts, and screws. And there were always a few old rolls of paper towels, oily rags, and miscellaneous tools left behind from projects long forgotten, electrical connectors of every type dating back for years and, lastly, the photos of past crews and good times stacked in the drawers and adhered to the interior walls.

As I exited the cabin and climbed down the ladder, I did a walk around to inspect her haul. She looked solid, with just a few water bubbles on her gel. She was light blue, and her name was boldly written in black letters acrost her stern, "*Genie*." I also noticed there were a few stanchions that were damaged along her port side and bow, but nothing serious.

The marina manager had been right. She was in pretty decent condition, being she was an abandoned sailboat. I didn't think it would take too much time or money to fix her up. More elbow grease than anything.

I returned to the marina office and told the manager that I was interested in *Genie*.

My wife did not know who *Genie* was, but she quickly joined our conversation. "*Genie*?" she exclaimed. "Who is *Genie*?"

I told her that there was a nice little sailboat in the boneyard. If the manager sold her to me for the right price, I would like to buy her and fix her up. I told my wife that I just wanted to know what the marina wanted for her. Then I figured the two of us would talk about the purchase later.

I directed my attention back to the manager who smiled, knowing there was going to be a serious discussion between my wife and I before this transaction could happen, but he was not going to make it too difficult for me. He knew he could put a big number on her, and I would walk away. This would take the heat off his employee—my wife—but he really did want this boat to make revenue for the marina and not go to the dump, as it cost the marina quite a bit of money to dispose of these old fiberglass boats. Besides, he was going to make some guy—me—happy if he sold the old boat for almost nothing.

He was still wiping the sweat from his forehead as he thought about how much to ask for her. Then he said that the marina had just spent sixty dollars to transfer the title and another month of land rent had accumulated, so he thought one hundred dollars would be a fair asking price.

I got a big smile on my face, knowing that one hundred dollars was well within my means and that it would be hard for my wife to argue that *Genie* was too expensive at that price.

But my wife is not just some person who is oblivious to the cost of boat storage. She worked at the marina. She dealt with collecting storage and dock rental fees all day long. She dealt with the vendors who billed the owners for all the work they did on the boats, so she was not sold immediately.

I kissed my wife then shook the marina manager's hand, telling him that I would have to discuss this further with my wife and make sure a boat was within my budget. That put the wife at ease. No rash decisions that she did not have some say in.

Then the manager told me if I left the boat where it was, in the boneyard, he would discount my rental fee, being he would not have to move her. Forty dollars a month was what he quoted me for the land storage. That was only four hundred eighty dollars a year. Not bad considering they provide power and water, and I could use the other marina facilities.

That evening, I worked it out with the wife and made all the necessary concessions so that she would permit me to buy the little sailboat named *Genie*. The following week, I visited the marina once again and met with the marina manager. Presenting my check in the amount of one hundred dollars, the title to *Genie* was handed over to me. I was now the new proud owner of a South Coast 23' sailboat.

Chapter Two:
The Cleanout

I could hardly wait to start working on *Genie*. The following weekend, I went to the marina and visited my wife, as usual. This time, I brought with me everything necessary to start cleaning *Genie* out. I figured that should be step one— just get the trash and endless assortment of cleaners and concoctions out of her belly.

At first glance, I thought this would only take me an hour or so, but I quickly realized that the summer heat made the temperatures inside *Genie* oppressively hot. This slowed my work down to a crawl. I would gather as much of her contents as I possibly could and toss them out of her manway. Then I spread the items out on her decks, sorting the matter into piles of trash and a small pile of keepers (the keepers being tools, hardware, or usable items that had been removed from her at one time or another). There was also the occasional discovery of treasure, those new items that had been purchased and stashed but never installed. *Genie* had a few of those, including a new bilge pump and switch.

I loaded all the trash I could into black plastic trash bags then hauled them to the yard's waste bin. This took the better part of my first day with *Genie*.

It was the following week when I really got into cleaning her. I removed her cushions from the berth and the extra sails that I found stowed in her cabin. I pulled the anchor, lines, and chain. Everything that could be moved was removed and loaded into my vehicle. Then I ran the hose and made buckets of soapy water. Inch by inch, I washed her inside, from bow to stern, with brushes and sponges. And not just the hull, but every part and component within her. Even the cabin ceiling had to be scrubbed. To remove the wastewater, I had to siphon it off with a smaller hose. Next, I cleaned her exterior and made sure her scuppers were clear.

As I washed *Genie*, I took inventory of her needs. She was old but solid. A modest girl, but she still had beautiful lines.

When I left the marina's boneyard that evening, after a full day in the sun, I knew *Genie* would sail once again. She had shown me her worst and, with all that, I still found myself loving her.

It was weeks before I could return to work on her, but I did not let that stop me. I washed her sails at my home and strung them from tree to tree to dry them out. I purchased new lanyards and parts that I would need to make her whole. There was also the matter of replacing her dead battery and installing a small solar array to keep it charged. I let all new items accumulate in my storage shed at the house, anticipating the installation of each.

It was now August, and as anyone from Maryland knows, it is hot and humid in the boatyard this time of year. Some days, there was absolutely no air movement at all. I really was not looking forward to crawling into *Genie's* cabin and doing any serious work until the heat broke. Instead, I focused on her exterior.

One by one, I replaced her halyards, taping the new ones to the existing then pulling them through each of her blocks. Having been a Boy Scout, I felt compelled to splice end-splices and eye-splices on all the lanyards about her deck. Then I focused on painting her with a fresh coat of paint made specifically for fiberglass.

After completely painting her hull with a semi-gloss white paint, I stood back and was awestruck by how much her appearance had changed. Like an ugly duckling maturing into a beautiful white swan, *Genie* had been transformed.

Next, I prepped her for the painting of her pinstripes, water lines, and bottom. I meticulously taped off her name and each line so as not to ruin her fresh white paint. Then, with a fine brush and a can of black gloss paint, I painted them in. This left the bottom to be painted. Her original bottom paint was blue, yet I had decided to paint it black.

As the summer drew to its conclusion, the cleanout of *Genie* came to an end, too.

Chapter Three:
Refinish & Repairs

As the summer was winding down and the temperatures started to cool, I turned my focus to the refurbishment of *Genie's* cabin. I resealed her cabin windows and refinished her teak with several coats of varnish. This included her tiller handle and seating boards in the cockpit. I installed a gray, indoor-outdoor carpet in her berth to soften the rough fiberglass finish that was typical of the old hulls. Then I installed a new battery and, with the flick of a switch, she came to life. Starboard, port, and mast lights all illuminated with a bright, warm glow. Her interior lights worked but seemed quite tattered.

To dress her up a bit, I purchased two new interior lights and mounted them; one in her berth and the other in the cabin. I added a marine radio and a compass to her navigation equipment, installing the radio just inside her cabin and the compass just outside the manway in her cockpit.

I installed a small-long shaft 1954 Seagull boat engine that I had been using on a small skiff that I had made. This small engine was almost the right era for her but not necessarily the most reliable engine in 2001. Besides, you had to wind the rope pull cord by hand to start it.

The last part of putting *Genie* together was reinstalling her anchor and sails and equipping her with all the necessary

Coast Guard required safety equipment. She now had a throw ring, air horn, life preservers, charts, and flares.

Genie had come together, one component at a time. Her days of being stranded on the hard in the boneyard were coming to an end.

It was now late September; this is a good time to sail the Chesapeake, and I was itching to give *Genie* a run. It's also the time of year that the boatyard starts to fill up as the fair-weather captains pull their boats and head for warmer seas.

PART II:
SEA TRIALS

Chapter Four:
Launch

Up to this point, I had paid for her land storage at the Anne Arundel County Marina every month without fail, but it was a time in my life when my family was relocating to Chesapeake Beach. This meant that *Genie* would be more than thirty minutes away if I left her in the Anne Arundel County Marina where I had rescued her.

There was a boatyard at Plum Point, Breezy Point Marina. It was just around the corner from my new home. I visited the marina and found that it was owned and operated by Mike Strandquist.

Mike was a little older than me, but he had also grown up in Annapolis. We had a lot in common, and we knew many of the same people and families. Like me, Mike was a seasoned sailor. He had his own sailboat on the hard in his marina, always telling me that he did not have time to sail her with his busy life, operating his marina. The adage, "the shoemaker wearing no shoes," was alive and well.

I decided to store *Genie* on the hard at Breezy Point that first winter. It was less expensive than the Anne Arundle County boatyard. I knew she would be at home there, being Plum Point's channel was relatively shallow. This restricted the boats using the marina to those having less than a three-foot draft. *Genie's* draft was about two-foot-ten, just shallow enough to make it through. Additionally, all sailboats entering the channel had to pass under the high powerlines that were at forty-two feet. *Genie's* mast was about twenty-seven feet high, so she could tuck in under the wires without any issues.

Plum Point Channel into Breezy Point Marina – overhead wires.

First things first, I had to get *Genie* to Breezy Point Marina, and you just don't take an unproven boat that has been at rest on the hard out on a voyage in the Chesapeake without a sea trial. So, I put in my order to have *Genie* launched and made arrangements to keep her in a slip for a couple of weeks. This would be the first time she had tasted the waters of the Chesapeake in years, so I really did not know what to expect. But I thought it would be wise to evaluate her before taking her into the open waters of the bay.

The yard crew launched her on a Friday afternoon. I was quite surprised that they just used a forklift to do the job, but it proved to be quick and painless. No rigging, straps, or issues maneuvering around the yard. As soon as they lifted her hull, black paint was applied where the four stands had held her in place for years. Within minutes, her bow was pointed toward the launching well, and she almost appeared to be flying into position.

As she settled in on the surface of the water, she was led away from the supporting forks of the lift. Now floating for the first time in years, she seemed like a small toy in a bathtub.

I boarded her while she was still in the launch well and made sure there were no leaks. I then installed her little British Seagull engine, started it up, and navigated her into her temporary slip. This little engine was only about 1 to 2 hp, but it was enough to move *Genie* around quite well in the still waters of Rockhold Creek. The only bad thing about this engine was that it did not have a reverse. Therefore, I had to spin it completely around to reverse it and hold the shaft down while doing so to prevent the prop from hitting the rudder. *Genie's* small engine well did not make this an easy task, but I figured it worked well enough, being one does not move a sailboat in reverse often.

After her launch and a short trip around the docks, I secured *Genie* in her slip with her new dock lines and called it a day. I figured I would spend some time with her the following day and take her on a short run up and down Rockhold Creek, or maybe just out of the creek in the channel, for her first sea trial if the weather cooperated.

The following day, as I walked the docks toward *Genie*, I could see her bilge was pumping water. This brought on a panic. There had been no apparent leak when I'd left her the day before, and being it had not rained that evening, I could not imagine what was going on.

I entered her cabin and quickly found the problem. The thru-hull valve for her sink was leaking under the bench seat in her main cabin. This was not good. I knew that *Genie's* battery would not hold up for long, being I did not have a charging system.

I sat and watched the leak for a while and found that the pump was having to turn on about once every thirty minutes to keep up with the leak.

Fortunately, my wife happened to be working that day, so I went to the office and told her about the leak, hoping she could find someone to help me fix *Genie* before she sank.

My wife knew all the venders at the marina and quickly made a call to Buster Phipps Boat Works Inc., one of the vendors who had experience in this type of work. I was told not to worry about it being fixed, that she would take care of it. So, I left the keys to *Genie's* cabin with the vendor then left the marina to complete a list of errands.

I was worried that *Genie* would be under water before long, and I was not sure how long the battery could keep her afloat. All I could imagine was the valve being pulled, and a geyser of water spouting up through her hull. I gave myself a good tongue-lashing about not having replaced the gaskets in that valve before her launch. It just hadn't occurred to me that such a small valve, that is almost never used, would be such a problem.

Within an hour or two, my wife called to inform me that the seals on the thru-hull valve had been replaced and the leak had been stopped. She also noted that I owed Mr. Phipps some money for the work.

It was the following day that I made a visit to the marina to inspect the repair work. I was truly amazed that the entire valve gasket repairs had been done with less than a cup of water leaking in.

I located Mr. Phipps, who had made the repair, thanked him, and paid him promptly. I asked him how he had done the repair without taking on a significant amount of water, and he just smiled at me and said, "Experience." Somehow, I knew that was all I was going to get out of him, so I left it at that, figuring it was some trade secret.

Being she was repaired, it was trial day. I decided to take *Genie* out of the channel and raise her sails. I wanted to see how she would handle and if there were any issues with her rigging before sailing her down to Breezy Point Marina.

I pulled her out of her berth, pointed her bow toward the channel, and hoisted her 130 genoa sail. With the 6-knot breeze coming across her port, the sail quickly filled and brought *Genie* to life. We sailed out of the marina on a port tack, and as I entered the channel, her stern passed through the direction of the wind, forcing me to jibe. I then resumed our course on a starboard tack, out of Rockhold Creek and into the bay. So as not to run her aground, I kept her in the channel.

After passing the last green channel marker, I then rounded the marker, changing course and heading almost due south in Herring Bay. About thirty minutes into the trial, I headed her upwind and brought the sail to a full luff. Then I quickly raised her mainsail and resumed our southward course, on a starboard tack, toward Herring Harbor South.

It did not take me long to realize that *Genie* was not the fastest boat on the bay, even with her main and a 130% genoa. Having raced 420 sailboats on the Severn River most of my youth, I was not accustomed to the feel and handling of a full-keeled, cruising-type boat that seemed to move at her own pace no matter how much I cursed. She had a top speed of about 6 knots, and I quickly found out that her freeboard was not really suitable for rough seas—the deck was getting wet, yet the seas were less than two feet during this initial run.

After reaching the outermost marker of Herrington Harbor South, I brought *Genie* around and headed due north, back up the channel, toward Rockhold Creek. She was on a broad reach port tack as I sailed her back. This was a smooth ride and even slower than her trip south, but it gave me some time to reflect on what had happened.

Genie had been reborn. She was now loved and sailing upon the waters of the Chesapeake once again. Both of our souls were smiling that day as she tackled each swell that met her bow, navigating back to her temporary berth.

Upon returning to Rockhold Creek, I lowered her mainsail and proceeded toward the docks with just her genoa.

It was a smooth approach. I almost felt like *Genie* was showing me that she could do it herself.

As we reached her slip, I pointed her bow into the wind and let her sheet go. Grabbing the pilings, I worked her in stern first so she was ready for a quick exit the next time out. Before leaving that day, I then plugged in a battery charger and set it to trickle, to replenish the lost charge from the bilge pump.

Chapter Five:
Relocated

Genie's time was up at the marina in Rockhold Creek. I now had to move her to Breezy Point. It was late September, or early November, as I recall, and the weather was getting unpredictable. I had a full-time job that only left me the weekends to deal with *Genie*. As with most fall days on the Chesapeake, the winds were getting stiff, and the temperatures had dropped quite a bit, making it necessary to wear a heavy jacket while out on the water. I was starting to wonder if I needed to bring someone else along to help me sail her the twelve miles, but I did not know anyone available, so I figured I would just do it myself. I expected that it would take about two hours total for the trip.

Breezy Point Marina with docks empty in the spring.

I had parked my vehicle at Breezy Point so I would not need a ride once I delivered *Genie* to the marina. I then had my wife pick me up at Breezy Point and take me to work with her that Saturday morning.

As before, I raised her genoa sail after pulling her out of her slip. However, this time, the winds were coming from a northerly direction, making it difficult to sail directly to the Rockhold Creek channel. Being surrounded by expensive boats and restricted channels, I decided to fire up the British Seagull.

I wound the starting cord and pulled. After a few attempts, it sprang to life, billowing a cloud of blue smoke. I powered her toward the channel and , all the while, the genoa sail was luffing in the breeze as I headed windward. I changed course to follow the channel into the bay, and the genoa sail filled, quickly outpowering the little British Seagull, so I shut down the Seagull and proceeded under sail power.

As I entered the Chesapeake, the winds were at about 15 knots, and the swells on the bay were about two to three feet. That was all the freeboard *Genie* had, so each wave was cresting her bow. She was also heeling quite a bit, and her starboard toe rail was running just atop the waterline as I proceeded out of the Rockhold Creek channel and into Herring Bay on a port tack.

I changed course once again and headed due south, toward Herrington Harbor South. The wind was now on my stern, and the seas were following me. This was awesome. *Genie* was exceeding her maximum hull speed, for sure, by having the water moving with us.

As I raced along, I ended up with a swell on *Genie's* stern that seemed to almost sit there, and another was in front of her bow. We were in a trough as we almost surfed to the last marker of Herring Bay before passing Herrington Harbor South's channel.

To experience such speed in a boat like *Genie* was a great rush, but I knew she was at her upper limit. She had been designed by Carl Alberg, who was recognized for his designs of stable crafts made for family cruising and comfortable accommodations. He expected his boats to sail upright without scaring the life out of family and friends. That's how he described his fifty-six boat designs.

As I rounded red marker #2, off of Fairhaven, I changed course once again to avoid the shallows off of Holland Point. I set a new course for green marker #1. This was about a one-and-a-half-mile distance. I remained on a port tack, and *Genie* started to take waves on her port side as we made way toward our new mark. It was at this time that I made a critical sailing error.

As I passed Herrington Harbor South, a larger sailboat emerged from the marina and, unknown to me, it was on a collision course with *Genie*. I could not see through my genoa sail and therefore had no idea this near-miss was about to happen. However, there was no way the other sailing vessel was not aware of me. He, too, was on a port tack but had right of way, being downwind and bearing his port side to me as he set his course. It was not until he passed my stern with about twenty feet of clearance did I even know he existed. But, apparently, he had to change his course to avoid the collision by almost heading directly into the wind.

This encounter left the captain, who I will refer to as Captain Clown from this point forward, upset. He visually signaled to me with his rude hand gestures that he was displeased with having to yield to avoid the collision.

I got on the radio and apologized for not having seen him in time to alter my course; however, this apology did not resolve the matter. He was obviously a racing sailor, and his boat was a fast J-105 with several hands on deck. He was not going to let me get away with that, even though *Genie* was a family cruiser.

He quickly fell off his mark and proceeded to set a parallel course with *Genie*. Within a few moments, he was overtaking *Genie* on her windward side.

Now, having raced boats in my youth, I knew the rules well, and I knew I could head him up to a luff if I wanted to. But this was not a race, and I had already pissed Captain Clown off. All I wanted to do was stay on my course and deliver *Genie* to Breezy Point Marina.

Captain Clown made it clear he was not going to be able to sleep at night until he got revenge. This was road rage on the water at its best.

As I navigated *Genie* toward the #1 green buoy, Captain Clown navigated to within ten feet of my port side. As he passed, he blanketed *Genie's* sail, causing her port side rail, which I was sitting on, to quickly go below water as her starboard side raised high above my line of sight. A good three-foot swell immediately entered *Genie's* cockpit and flooded it within seconds. I found myself standing on the sides of the port cockpit seats, reaching for the starboard side as *Genie* swallowed the first wave. Much of the water went into the cabin manway as *Genie* righted herself. Then the heavy wind hit her genoa sail as Captain Clown passed. The sail made a popping sound as it quickly filled and pulled her starboard rail down to the water line again. I maneuvered as quickly as possible, through the cockpit that was full of water, back to the port cockpit seat, and attempted to navigate *Genie* back on course.

Well, well, Captain Clown and his motley crew had gotten their revenge at the cost of getting me wet. They should have been happy with that.

It took me about fifteen minutes to fully recover. Fortunately, *Genie* had not suffered any physical damage, though her pride was most definitely hurt.

I thought Captain Clown had gotten his fill of revenge and would sail off, but no. That apparently had not satisfied his rage.

As I moved just south of buoy marker #1, I looked upwind to see the J-boat heading back my way. I changed course and set my new heading to about 165 degrees south-southeast, toward yellow nun 7B. That would be about a three-nautical-mile run and, on an average day, it would have taken *Genie* about thirty minutes to cover the distance.

After a short period of time, Captain Clown and his J-boat were back, quickly passing *Genie* on her starboard side, but at least twenty boat lengths away. As he proceeded on his course between *Genie* and Holland Point, I lost sight of him again behind *Genie's* genoa sail. This was truly an unsettling feeling—knowing the larger sailboat was going to have to cross my path once again to avoid running into the shallows.

On this tack, *Genie* made good time as she settled back into a trough with following winds and seas. I used the tiller extension and made my way to her downwind, starboard cockpit seat. I raised the genoa to see where Captain Clown was, and there he was, in the process of making a course change to put his boat on another collision course with *Genie*. This time, I was ready for him, being I knew he was there, and just let *Genie's* sails out a little further so she slowed down.

The seas started to roll under her instead of running along in a trough. I kept her going forward just enough so she would not breach. This left Captain Clown in the position of having to either stop his J-boat and wait for me or continue to race by. He chose to race by, well ahead of *Genie*, crossing her course not less than ten boat lengths away. To actually hit *Genie* or cause me to change course, he would have had to change tack and head for her, but that would have given me the right of way. Captain Clown was not about to cause a collision with his fine racing boat, giving up his right of way, so he sailed off in the direction of Knapp Narrows, most likely heading to St. Michaels, never to be seen by me again.

Now that Captain Clown was gone, I restored *Genie's* sail to power her up to her full potential.

Genie was in the trough again as we approached yellow nun 7B on *Genie's* port side, passing the Rod and Reel and Fishing Creeks entrance on *Genie's* starboard. Within minutes, we were passing the US Navy Research Laboratory Annex with its red and white antenna array.

I then set course for green can #1 that was due south of yellow nun 7B. This was approximately four more miles. *Genie* should have been able to sail this in forty-five minutes on a good day, but today, we could easily do it in thirty minutes or less.

Genie did an exceptional job of sailing that leg of the trip. We passed the Willows Colony Beach and, before long, I could see Breezy Point Park and Campground along the beach as we approached the Plum Point channel. I now had to jibe to bring *Genie* into Plum Point Creek's channel, which was not necessarily the easiest action with a large genoa sail but absolutely necessary.

As soon as I brought her around and set her course into Plum Point Creek, I wound the rope around the British Seagull head and started it. The little British Seagull engine's prop was barely touching the water. With each swell, the prop splashed the water upon entering, and then again as the swell rolled by and the prop exited the water again. The little British Seagull had no neutral, so I just let it run as slow as I could. Then, upon entering the channel, I dropped *Genie's* sail, gathered it upon her deck, grabbed the tiller, and guided her toward Breezy Point Marina.

Genie had made it to what would be her new home, wet but unscathed by the day's events. I brought her to rest in the launch well where Mike had asked me to dock her.

Chapter Six:
Final Touches

Within the week, *Genie* was pulled and set up for winter storage. Mike had *Genie* packed in tight with several other sailboats similar in size at the end of the marina harbor. Breezy Point is more of a powerboat, fisherman's launch kind of marina, but sailing was a passion of Mike's, so he treated the sailors with respect.

I spent the winter putting the final touches on *Genie*. Her damaged stanchions and bow rail were replaced, and a new toe rail was installed where a failing one had started to come apart.

In January of 2002, I arranged to rent a slip for *Genie* at Breezy Point Marina. It was on the far side of the marina, just a few slips down from the boat launch ramp. It was not a slip I would have normally selected, but it was one of the few slips open for rental. Mike always gave the previous slip renters first choice and the option to keep a slip if they liked it. New renters had a choice of the open slips, if there were any, so I selected the deepest water slip he had available that was in my price range.

During this period, when *Genie* was resting on the hard, I had her repowered. This included new sails and a new engine. I was not sure what type of engine I should get, but the British Seagull was lacking a reverse gear, locking shaft, self-recoiling pull cord, and was extremely low on horsepower. I felt I needed something a little more dependable and with a few modern features.

Winter proved to be a good time to shop for this type of engine, so I searched the local Penny Saver advertisements, figuring a four or five horsepower engine with reverse would work better if I could find one at the right price, and I found a four horsepower Mercury for sale in Annapolis for three hundred dollars.

I visited the engine repair shop that was selling it and ended up buying it on the spot after the mechanic demonstrated that it ran. He told me that he had just replaced the impeller, and it should be good for years to come, provided I winterize it properly.

Next, I went in search of new sails. After endless hours of shopping online, I decided to go with North Sails. They seemed to be highly rated and offered me the best bang for the buck.

I carefully made measurements for each sail and decided to go with a 120 genoa instead of the 130 genoa that had come with *Genie*. I felt the 130 might be good for light air during the summer but was too much for heavy air that was typical in the spring and fall sailing season. Besides, I had planned on keeping the original sails, so I always had the option of using them if the replacement sails were not the right combination.

It took about six weeks for the sails to be delivered. It was now February or early March. I took the sails down to the marina and loaded them into *Genie*. With just a light wind blowing, I raised the new sails and let them luff in the breeze.

When Mike saw what I had done, he quickly ran over and asked me to lower the sails. One mistake, just one shift in the wind or gust, and *Genie* would have come down off her stands and taken out half the boats around her in a domino effect. I knew he was right, so I quickly took them down, folded them, rolled them, and stowed them in *Genie's* cabin.

PART III:
Voyage to the Volvo Race Start

Chapter Seven:
Spring Launch

It was the first week in April 2002 that I put in an order to have *Genie* launched at Breezy Point Marina. Mike was not one to mess around, so just a day or two after placing the order, she was moved into her slip. With rockfish season starting May 1st, I was sure Mike wanted to get as many launches as possible out of the way, as all the fishermen would be putting their orders in the last two weeks of April.

My goal for such an early launch was to sail *Genie* north to Annapolis for leg seven of the Volvo—around the world races that were to start on April 28, 2002 at the Chesapeake Bay Bridge. I had myself all pumped up.

Aerial Photo of Annapolis Harbor – Bay Bridge upper left, Severn River on left, East Port and East Port Bridge right center, Back Creek to right, and further to the right, out of photo, is Lake Ogleton.

As the racers crossed the finish line of leg six, Miami to Baltimore, 875 nautical miles on April 17, 2002, Team News Corp had won. I was kind of down about that because I was actually cheering for the German boat, *Illbruck Challenge*, skippered by John Kostecki, an American from Pittsburg, Pennsylvania.

I made several trips to Annapolis after the racers had arrived and visited the various boats as they were put on display at the city docks. It was incredible to see these boats in person with their long keels and distinct racing sails.

In order to make it to the start of the Volvo Race, I figured I would have to sail *Genie* up to Lake Ogleton. Then, from there, sail to the starting line in the early morning of April 28th. This was too long of a run to do in just one day.

I set my itinerary as *Genie* sat in her slip at Breezy Point. I planned on sailing from Breezy Point to Rockhold Creek on April 26th. I also planned on sleeping that evening aboard *Genie*. Then, the following morning, I planned on sailing from Rockhold Creek to Lake Ogleton. I figured I would spend the night of April 27th aboard *Genie* and, at morning's first light, I would sail out to the starting line near the Chesapeake Bay Bridge.

I figured that, even if I did not make it to the starting line in time to witness the actual start, I would still see all the boats as they headed south in the bay. I then figured I would sail *Genie* back to Rockhold Creek that same day and lastly sail her to Breezy Point on April 29th.

My itinerary was set. I made all the necessary arrangements to take off work from April 26 through May 3, 2002. I had the trip completely planned out, and *Genie* was ready to sail.

Chapter Eight:
Leg One to Herring Bay

As my wife got ready to commute to work the morning of April 26th, I had her drop me off at Breezy Point Marina with basic provisions for the trip. Thursday the 25th had had decent weather with the winds coming out of the south most of the morning; however, the winds had switched over to north-northwest by midday and had gotten quite gusty by mid-afternoon.

As I unloaded the gear, said my goodbyes to my wife, and then walked over to *Genie's* slip, I noticed the winds were light and coming out of the west-southwest.

I loaded *Genie*, mounted her motor, and filled the fuel tank. I then turned on her electric power switch and released her from the mooring lines.

She was floating freely in her slip, but the water and winds were so calm that she did not move. Having been trained on smaller sailboats, without the luxury of an engine to rely upon, I was reluctant to use one. Having no choice, however, I pulled on the engine starter rope, and the little Mercury fired up, breaking the morning silence. I quickly locked it into forward, and we started off on our expedition.

Genie left only a small wake as we traveled out of the marina and headed into the channel for open waters. Once we passed under the power lines and I cleared the campground, we entered the open waters of the Chesapeake. A slight breeze could then be felt on my back, coming out of the west.

I shut down the engine and hoisted *Genie's* genoa sail. Then, while it luffed in the breeze, I raised the mainsail. Pulling in her sheets and cleating each into position, I brought *Genie* into a north heading and locked her tiller into place. I was on a port tack, and her sails were full, but the air was so light that our speed was slow.

It was one of those mornings on the bay when you felt that God had put everything there just for you. The seas were flat with just an occasional ripple, it was quiet and serene, and it gave me time to appreciate what I had and what a beautiful planet I lived on. It was a time when I felt I could whisper to God, and He would hear me loud and clear. So, I made sure I gave thanks for the day.

There were a few birds on the wing, making their way across my path, and I saw a few others bobbing in the water as the sun grew higher in the sky. There were so few boats on the bay that day that I don't recall seeing any move until midday. Then, like a mirage off in the distance, I witnessed a large sailboat making its way south in the far channel along the eastern shore. This channel runs parallel with the western shore channel and is about four or five miles west from the channel I was in.

First, only its dark maroon sails could be seen. Then, as it proceeded south, I could just make out the hull above the water line for a few moments before watching her fade away.

It had been about two hours, and I had only been able to travel about two miles north of Plum Point. Fortunately for me, the winds started to pick up a little as the day went on. By noon, I had made it to Holland Point. Winds had shifted to south-southwest, which allowed me to head north-northwest, toward Rockhold Creek, without having to make any major changes to the sails.

I ate my first lunch aboard *Genie* that day as I kept watch, adjusting our heading on occasion as I drifted off my bearing from the motion of the waves and tides. The temperature had been between 50 and 60° Fahrenheit all day. It was a pleasant sail, uneventful by any standard, and by two p.m., I was entering Rockhold Creek and heading for the transient slip that I had rented for the evening.

My original plan was to spend the night on *Genie* that first night, but my wife had convinced me to spend the night at home so I would be fresh for leg two. I yielded to her request and left everything on *Genie* that night, including the little engine, secured into its position. Only the genoa was completely removed and stored in the bow locker. I then locked the cabin and left *Genie* for the night.

That evening, I asked my son if he would like to join me for the balance of the expedition. I figured it would be a good opportunity to bond with my teenage son and share with him the pleasures associated with sailing. He agreed to join me; however, it did take a little coaxing, as I recall.

The second leg, from Rockhold Creek to Lake Ogleton, was just about the same distance as the first leg of my venture. However, this time, I knew we would be spending the night aboard *Genie* then heading out to the Volvo Races that following morning at sunrise. This would be more like a camping trip than just a sailing adventure.

I had my son pack a change of clothes and a few additional rations so he would have what he needed to complete the trip. I also added a couple of fishing poles to our provisions so we could try to catch a couple panfish for dinner.

Chapter Nine:
Leg Two to Lake Ogleton

It was Saturday, April 27th. The wife dropped both my son and myself off at the marina. As we walked the pier to *Genie's* slip, it was a chilly morning, about 35 to 40° Fahrenheit, making the thought of heading out on the open water much less appealing than during the summer. The winds were coming out of the east at about 10 knots. This would make our exit from the marina and Rockhold Creek a little more difficult than it had been getting in the prior day.

I was forced to rely on the engine once again to leave the marina and to exit the Rockhold Creek channel. Technically, I could have tacked back and forth to head upwind and eventually sailed *Genie* out of the creek, but *Genie* had a full keel, and the channel servicing Rockhold Creek is quite narrow, with extremely shallow waters on both sides. It was not worth the risk of getting grounded and having the entire adventure spoiled just so I could boast that I sailed her out of the marina.

As we cleared the last of Rockhold Creek's channel markers, I set a course south-southeast. I had my son take the tiller as I hoisted *Genie's* genoa and mainsails. Then I cut the engine and trimmed the sails, showing my son how to maximize their output. I was on a port tack once again, but this time, we were getting farther away from our destination, mainly to avoid running aground on Herring Bay's sandbar that was between us and the deeper waters of the Chesapeake. We also took this bearing because the wind required us to either head northerly or southerly, being the winds were mostly out of the east and northeast. The sandbar restricted our path northward, so a southerly course was our only option if we were going to sail out of Herring Bay.

As we passed green marker #3, I changed course and headed easterly, as close to the wind as *Genie* would go. This was still well out of our way, but the shallows were deep enough at this point to permit *Genie* to cross without running aground.

After we crossed the sandbar, I tacked and set a course for about 30° northeast, putting us on a starboard tack. This was the first tack my son had experienced, and it was difficult to explain that he needed to release the genoa sheets on one side then work the sail around the mast to the leeward side of the boat, all the while making sure to duck and not let his head get hit by the changing boom. Then he needed to grab the sheets on the genoa and pull them in again to catch the wind on the new tack, all while turning the boat with the tiller.

Now, to an experienced sailor, this all sounds boring and almost automatic, like riding a bike. But, to a young guy, having never experienced the maneuver before, this was a set of daunting tasks—while the only thing on his mind was that the boat was now heeling on the opposite side from where he was sitting, and he needed to get to the higher side of the boat. For my son to have his father calling out commands, like, "Watch your head," "Release the line," "Get the sail around the mast," and then command him to "Get the downwind genoa sheet and pull it in before it's lost," this was not something he had expected. But after we had completed the maneuver and started to make way, he quickly understood the processes and seemed to smile at the complexities of sailing versus a power boat. Or, I should say, this was what I read of his facial expressions.

The winds had remained light that day but, in retrospect, it was probably a blessing being I had a landlubber on board. Unfortunately, the temperatures remained quite cool and left us with a chill on our cheeks and noses.

As midday approached, I set course for Thomas Point Lighthouse. The winds had started to come from more of a southeasterly direction, and we started to make better time.

Continuing a starboard tack, we rounded Thomas Point around two p.m. that afternoon.

The winds were still light, but the temperature had warmed up a bit, into the low 60s. I changed our heading to Tolly Point green marker 1AH. That was a two-mile run from the lighthouse, but as we fell off some from the windward mark, we were able to pick up a little more speed.

In less than an hour, we rounded 1AH. I then set our new course to the green marker #1 at the entrance to Lake Ogleton's channel.

It was about four p.m. when we reached the main channel marker. I knew we had to jibe to enter the lake's channel, so I gave my son the order to duck and stay down as I pulled the tiller hard and pulled in the mainsail so it would not whip across the entire boat cockpit and slam into the other side. As the boat changed course to a west-southwest direction, I slowly released the main again then ordered my son to release the genoa sail sheet and bring the genoa around the mast before I trimmed the sails. It was a picture-perfect jibe, and we were on course to enter Lake Ogleton.

Having grown up in Annapolis Roads, I was familiar with all the idiosyncrasies of this lake and knew that the best place to anchor for the evening was just inside the lake entrance, on the starboard side, next to the beach and red marker #4, for the night. I called my wife to let her know our status. She convinced me to meet her at the Annapolis Roads community pier, telling me that she had a special treat for us.

I proceeded into the pier and waited for her. She was happy to see that we had made the trip unscathed, and she presented us with an assortment of cheeseburgers, fries, and soda for dinner. We ate our dinner on the pier then said our goodbyes. It was getting late, and the sun set just before eight p.m. this time of year.

This was going to be my first overnight in *Genie*. I had dreamed about this moment ever since I'd started working on her. I did not want to be late. I also really had been looking forward to spending some time with my son, one on one.

I returned to the lake entrance again, this time under power. I was not about to tack for two hours in the dark to get to my planned mooring location.

I set the anchor and gave the anchor line enough slack to account for the changing tides. We set out a few fishing hooks in hopes of catching a fish or two, as I recall. And as I remember it, that did not pan out, but it was nice to just spend a little time with my son, doing something relaxing as I shared stories of my youth on the lake. I told him how I had fished the lake for soft crabs and panfish most of my childhood. I pointed out the beach that was just a few yards away from our mooring spot, Lands End Beach. It was where my friends and I would swim in the summer and beach our boats while water skiing on the lake. My soul was at home on this lake, and I felt completely secure spending the night there as *Genie* rocked us to sleep.

Chapter Ten:
Volvo Race Start

I awoke early in the morning of April 28th to the patter of rain on *Genie's* cabin. Having slept like a rock, I felt refreshed and ready to go, but as I poked my head out of the hatch, I could not see anything. It took me a few minutes to get oriented. The fog was as thick as a bowl of cream of crab soup. I could not even see the red channel marker just a few yards away. I thought to myself, *This is going to be a real challenge.*

I woke my son and made a cup of coffee. I thought it would be wise to wait some time before pulling up anchor to see if the fog would clear. The winds were blowing at about 10 to 15 knots out of the south. The temperature was about 60°, but because of the rain, it was chilly, and the thought of sailing out into the bay with such limited visibility was menacing.

After a quick breakfast, we put on our foul weather gear and made our way up to the cockpit. With the utmost concentration and squinting, I could make out the shadows of two additional boats that had apparently moored not far from ours sometime during the night. I assumed they were planning on doing the same thing as I was.

I tidied up *Genie* the best I could as we waited to see if the fog would lift. I fueled up the little outboard just in case it was needed.

As the sun came up higher in the sky, the visibility did increase a bit. Unfortunately, not as much as I would like. The rain had not let up, and the foggy rain event was jeopardizing the entire venture. If I could not see the start through the fog, this endeavor would be a complete failure.

About eight a.m., I figured it was a now-or-never moment. The other boats that had been mooring next to us were starting to get underway. Additionally, many of the other folks who had boats in Lake Ogleton, who had planned on attending the start, were filing out of the channel and into the bay, toward the Bay Bridge.

I pulled up the anchor and fired up *Genie's* engine. Turning on her running lights, I then pulled her into the channel to exit the lake.

As soon as we cleared the last marker, I set a course 60° northeast. Then I handed the tiller over to my son while I hoisted *Genie's* genoa sail then cut the engine. I chose to keep the mainsail under cover and not use it. I did not think it would add to our speed enough to justify the work required to manage it. We were on a broad starboard tack with the seas hitting us on the starboard transom, not normally considered bad sailing conditions.

As we progressed into the deeper waters of the Chesapeake, it became apparent that *Genie* was not built for this type of sailing. Waves were coming over her gunwales and into the cockpit. I could see the last green channel marker fade away fast in the dense fog as I held my course. I tried to keep our course steady so I would be able to find our way back if necessary. *Genie* was not equipped with any location-finding technology. No LORAN or GPS systems were on board, and mobile phones were not smart at the time. *Genie* was only equipped for visual navigation.

As we progressed toward the Bay Bridge, I started to see a large number of boat shadows passing before us from port to starboard, and I could hear their engines rumble in the distance. As we got closer, I realized the boats were in a line, coming out of Back Creek and the Severn River, heading more easterly than I was. Apparently, they, too, were heading out to see the start of the race. The biggest difference was that they were much larger than *Genie*, and they were not sailboats but power boats or, I should say, yachts.

We found ourselves in a bad place, and I had put us there. The wakes of the larger boats adding to the waves that were now three to four feet high were considered heavy for *Genie*. Enveloped by dense fog, cold rain, and crossing the paths of many larger crafts, this trip had become life threatening. Yes, as a sailboat, we had right of way, but I always believe in that old lesson about being dead right. That is, you can be right, have right of way, and it is one hundred percent the other guy's fault and still die. Better to yield and live another day than to be dead right.

I had been holding my course now for more than an hour and dodged more than one close call when I decided to give up and head back to the safety of Lake Ogleton. I figured that even if we made it out to the racing path, and I had no way of knowing where that was, we would not be able to see anything in this weather. On top of that, the chances of an accident with a yacht in this fog was so great that I could no longer justify the voyage.

My son had already retreated to the cabin after receiving a blow to the head from the swinging boom. He was now sitting on *Genie's* cabin floor, just looking up out of the manway at me. He was not enjoying this. He was wet, cold, and scared. His eyes told me that he wanted out. Even though he did not say so, I could clearly read it on his face.

PART IV:
Survival Trip Home

Chapter Eleven:
Safety of the Lake

I yelled down to him that we were going to head back to the safety of the lake, explaining that it was too foggy and dangerous to proceed.

He did not say a word. He just nodded.

I turned *Genie* into the wind and pulled her genoa around her mast, putting us into a port tack. It was going to be hard to sail her back and find the channel marker. I also had to contend with the loss of visibility from the genoa sail blocking my view of oncoming boats. With this realization, I asked my son to help me out by just being a lookout on the starboard side. Fortunately, most of the boats that had been heading out from the Severn and Back Creek had already passed the point that intersected our course. However, there were the stragglers, and they were trying to make up time. The worst part of this was now *Genie* was being hit with the steady pounding of three- and four-foot waves on her bow, each splashing across her deck and into the cockpit. The scuppers seemed to be handling most of it, and I don't believe the bilge pump came on more than a few times. But we were in ankle-deep water and being hit in the face with a splash of salt water several times a minute.

I recall seeing three or four yachts and large boats pass us as we made our way back to the lake. I believe most had radar and were able to avoid us as they sped by. Once we finished crossing this parade, we were in the quieter waters between Back Creek and Lake Ogleton. This was when it got a little scary.

Where are we? was all I could think, but I did not want to scare my crew, so I just kept looking for a channel marker, keeping my other eye on the compass. I had us on a heading of 240° east-southeast. It had been hours since we'd left the lake, and we were cold, wet, and beaten.

I looked down at my watch. It was almost noon, and I still had not seen any markers or land. Then, suddenly, out of nowhere, a green marker was within twenty feet of my bow. I could not believe it. It was the outermost marker of Lake Ogleton.

Despite all my misery, I had to smile as I pointed it out to my son, telling him that it was just where I'd left it. It had not moved. He did not seem impressed, but I was. To this day, I am not sure how we found ourselves so close to that marker. I was sure we were going to end up grounding *Genie* on Bembe Beach or Carr's Beach.

We entered the lake under sail, and as we passed through the channel, I called my wife. As I heard the words leave my lips, telling my wife that we had to abandon our journey, I felt utter defeat and despair. I had failed to accomplish the one thing I had set out to do—witness the start of leg seven of the 2002 Volvo Race. I had failed to show my son what a great sailor I was or to teach him how to sail. I was literally wet and washed up. I had failed.

But life is full of failures and successes and, being a positive person, I put the failure in perspective and was happy that I had spent some time with my son on an adventure. I had taken *Genie* from the boneyard to the bay, and she had thanked me for my hard work by keeping us safe in conditions much worse than she was made to endure.

We headed for the Annapolis Roads community dock where my wife brought us a lunch. Afterward, I asked my son, who was now somewhat seasick, if he wanted to go home with his mother. He gave a quick, "Yes," and was in the car before I could say another word. He'd had his fill of sailing, and I couldn't say I blamed him. I kind of wanted to get in the car myself, but this was my planned adventure, and I was going to finish it.

Chapter Twelve:
Dash to West River

I had planned on sailing back to Breezy Point, if possible. If not, then to at least Rockhold Creek. That was going to be tough with the winds coming from the south as they were.

As I headed back onto the lake, I waved goodbye to my wife and son and fired up *Genie's* engine. The fog was now starting to clear. I thought to myself, *Right, go figure. The race start is over; no need for fog now.*

I headed back out into the bay under power, knowing I would be taking a pounding to get *Genie* back home. Once we were in deeper waters, I raised her genoa sail and pointed her on a southeasterly course of 120°.

It was about one p.m. now, and I thought I should be able to make it to Rockhold Creek in a few hours if the winds held up. But the southerly winds and waves just pounded *Genie* hour after hour. By three p.m., the winds were pushing 25 mph, and the temperature was in the mid-70s. We had been on a starboard tack and heading as close to the wind as possible on *Genie*. I don't believe she was able to point any higher into the wind. The waves were starting to reach the five- and six-foot level as I rounded Thomas Point Lighthouse and changed to a port tack. I thought it might be wise to head up the South River to seek shelter, but due to the direction of the winds and waves, I knew I would have to go a great distance up the river to find the shelter I needed. I knew if I could make it to West River, I would be safer sooner.

I decided to dash to West River. *Genie* was well built, but she did not have the freeboard to handle seas with a chop of three feet or more. The winds were blowing so hard that the genoa cam cleat would not hold the sheet. I was forced to hold the sheet with my left hand and the tiller in my right as I navigated her toward Rhode River and West River.

The waves continued to come over the bow, the seas were pounding, and the winds were well beyond the tiny boat's design. But she held together with just the occasional crash in the cabin of some unfortunate item that had come dislodged. Her rigging was holding up, and her new sails were strong enough to withstand the pressure. I just kept a hand on the sheet and pulled the tiller for what seemed to be an eternity, keeping her on course for the river entrance.

The marine weather alert had been sounding out of the marine radio all afternoon. Small craft advisories were out on the bay, and there was a tornado warning for Southern Maryland. I was not really worried about the tornado, being I had never seen one, but the small craft warning was obvious, and the stability of *Genie* was iffy at best. If anything went wrong, just one small event, *Genie* would be lost, and I might be lost with her.

The waters of the Chesapeake were unforgiving this time of year. The bay's waters were still cold from the winter's chill, and any prolonged exposure would cause hypothermia. I had to be careful not to be knocked overboard, or to lose the sheet or tiller. Just one slip, and *Genie* might breach and capsize.

I had my life jacket on, and if you knew me, you would know that this was a sign that my life was in jeopardy. I even tied a lanyard around my waist just in case I got knocked overboard. I would be able to pull myself back onto *Genie*. The bad part of that was if I was knocked out and *Genie* went down, I would go with her.

I was sailing fast with just the genoa sail. In less than an hour, I had made it up into the mouth of West River. I was somewhat unfamiliar with the river. I had the charts and knew that it was relatively small, but it was not until I started heading upstream that I realized just how restrictive it was.

I had a relatively narrow channel to navigate, and once I was out of the heavy seas and into somewhat sheltered waters, I decided to use the motor to head up to Galesville. I dropped the genoa sail and started up the little motor. From there, I followed the channel markers until I reached an abandoned dockside restaurant. This would be my safe haven for the night.

I headed into one of the many empty slips and secured *Genie* for the evening. After assuring myself that she was stable, I went below deck to assess the damage that the hours of relentless pounding had caused. To my disbelief, there was no damage to the craft, but my toolbox had released most of its contents into the cabin where they had bounced around, making the most threatening sounds.

It was about five p.m. when I secured *Genie* in a slip for the night. I called in and reported my location to my wife then prepared dinner. The winds were really howling now, even in the sheltered river. Fortunately for me, the body of water was so small that the waves on the river were no more than a rough ripple.

I did my best that evening to clean up the cabin and secure all the loose items, returning each to its proper place in preparation for tomorrow's return to Breezy Point. I secured *Genie's* sails in the forward berth then rolled out my sleeping bag in the cabin berth.

Chapter Thirteen:
Final Run to Breezy Point

I awoke the morning of April 29th surprisingly refreshed and ready to go. I walked the dock and went to the abandoned restaurant, having seen some life within the building. I knocked on the door, and an older gentleman answered, stating that the place was closed. I explained that I understood the place was closed, but I wanted to know if I owed anything for the dockage last night. He told me not to worry; he figured that I had taken shelter from the storm, and he was good with it. I thanked him then proceeded back to *Genie* and made ready for my final run to Breezy Point.

I put together a breakfast of instant coffee and a muffin that my wife had packed. I did one final check of the boat and her rigging then brought the genoa sail up on the deck, hooked in her tack. The genoa sail now lay gathered on the deck with the halyard hooked to the head and the luff hooked into the forestay, ready to hoist. I debated on the use of the mainsail, but being the winds were so light, I thought I better plan on using it this leg of my trip.

The sun was out, the winds seemed light and somewhat nondirectional, but generally west-northwesterly. Having *Genie* backed into her slip made departure easy. I gathered her dock lines and stored them below deck then pushed us out of the slip. I went forward to the mast and hoisted the genoa first.

After cleating it into position, I raised the mainsail and made some adjustments to the boom vang. I checked the battens to make sure they were in their proper positions then hoisted the mainsail. I then made a few minor adjustments to the outhaul and pointed my bow toward the channel to exit the West River. I recall the winds being so light that I thought I might have to fire up the little engine just to get out of the river.

As *Genie* slowly made her way up the channel, we were underway—making way, as they say—but her heading was so close to the wind that I had trouble keeping her sails full. I had to fall off from the wind, gather a little speed, and then head up again.

Eventually, I came to the point in the river where the West River meets the Rhode River and the direction of the channel heads almost east to west. I continued on a port tack, just letting my sails way out to catch the wind.

I recall how pleasantly surprised I was to find myself with such favorable sailing conditions. After all, I could have easily perished the day before in the stormy weather. And after such a slow, puffy start to the trip, I was not even sure if I would be able to sail this final leg back to Breezy Point. In retrospect, I would have been much better off staying at port, but that was not obvious at the time.

I had to clear the channel by getting past green marker 1A before heading out to the main channel (I believe the main channel marker number is 87A, but I have not been back out there to confirm, and the marker numbers are not listed on my old charts). I was working with a 1993 chart book. I decided there would be no cutting through the shallows off Horseshoe Point this day. The charts had indicated that there was a depth of four feet, but with the hundreds of lost crab pots and known wrecks on the sholes, I figured it was not worth the risk.

It was just as I rounded the 1A marker and changed my heading to about 110° southeast that I was unexpectedly hit with the start of what would be the most life-threatening boat trip I have ever made. I should have noticed that, even though the seas were calm surrounding *Genie*, I could see white caps off in the near distance. I had written it off as a chop from the changing tides out in the channel and the heavy rains of yesterday. It had never dawned on me that I had been sailing in sheltered waters.

Just as I performed a jibe, as the boom swung over my head and put *Genie* on a starboard tack, the wind hit the sails like a baseball bat hitting your skull. A giant *pop!* sound cracked as the sails filled with fury and the sheets went taut. Everything slammed at one time.

Now, I know that one must be careful anytime you jibe in heavy wind, but when I started the jibe, there had just been a light breeze. Yet, before I could complete the pull on the tiller to make the jibe, the wind hit at 25 mph, or greater. The seas immediately started to increase and, within minutes, I found myself in a five- to seven-foot, white-capped chop. The waves were striking *Genie* on her port side stern as I headed for marker 87A.

Apparently, the river channel had been sheltered from the northwest winds, and now that I was out far enough in the bay that the winds were coming past Saunders Point, unobstructed with the seas churning upward, they struck the shallows of the Wild Grounds. As soon as I figured I had cleared the shallows, I now thought it would be best to head due south for channel marker 85A.

As I fell off my course toward 87A and set a new heading toward Marker 85A, the waves started splashing up through the engine well, over the gunwales, and into the cockpit. I was taking on water faster than the scuppers could let it out of the cockpit, and a bucket of water was entering the cabin with each wave.

I pulled on the tiller with all my might to keep my heading, and as I fought waves and seas with my left hand, I held the main sheet with my right. With the unrelenting winds blowing at 25 mph and wind gusts of more like 30 mph, I found myself with too much sail. *Genie* did not have a furling system for the headsail, and I had no way of just stopping and dropping the sails. With no crew on board, I had limited ability at this point to furl the sails.

Genie's full keel was now at the surface of the bay, with her mast spreaders almost touching the surface of the water. Her sails were set almost all the way out, with the boom and genoa both getting wet as each wave touched the sheets. I was now standing on the leeward side of the cockpit seats as I worked her tiller, attempting to make the 85A marker.

It had crossed my mind that it might just be easier and safer to head straight downwind, toward the eastern shore, but I knew that the waves would be even greater as the waters grew deeper and had time to build as they crossed the bay. So, I decided to continue my fight to stay the course.

After fighting for some time, I realized that I now had no choice—I had to point *Genie* into the wind and get the genoa down. I needed to put her into irons, as they say.

I let the tiller go hard to port, and as I did, *Genie's* bow headed into the wind, her stern sunk low in the passing wave trough as the first wave washed completely over the cockpit, filling it to the brim with water. I was now mid-drift in water as I sat in the cockpit, avoiding the boom as it approached my head. The mainsail swung violently to and fro as I attempted to pull in all the mainsheet slack. I then cleated the main sheet in place and attempted to take down the genoa as the seas lapped over her bow once every few seconds, and the genoa slapped violently in the wind, knocking me into the stanchion lines and post. Now, a 120 genoa headsail does not stop at the mast. No, on this boat, it proceeded all the way back to the cockpit. I was now clinging to one of the stanchions so as to not go overboard as I retreated to the cockpit and searched for a line that I could use to tie myself off to the boat.

First things first, I put on the life jacket and strapped it tight, thinking I would need it, as I would most likely have to drift all the way across the bay with little probability of being able to swim against the heavy seas. I was operating in knee-deep water as I eventually found a secure line to tie off with. But, like so many things in my life, nothing came easy.

I tried to move forward once again to reach the mast but, by now, *Genie's* bow had fallen off her windward mark, and she was starting to point north as the wind almost flattened her. I found myself spread eagle on her mainsail, having been tossed from the cockpit seat and into the sail. The genoa sail sheets had gotten knotted up on the mast cleats and formed the most perfect sail for catching wind. So much so that *Genie* was now on a port tack, heading northerly, with a mainsail cleated almost flat, and the genoa pulled in about halfway. I had to get the genoa down, or *Genie* and I were going to do deep sea diving.

I worked my way off of the mainsail, toward the mast. Then, with all my might, I untangled the genoa sheet from the cleats, letting the sail fly free. That was enough to allow *Genie* to right herself, and the bow started to point back into the wind enough that I could un-cleat the genoa and pull it down.

Nothing comes easy. Did I already say that? Okay, I will say it again. Pulling in the genoa was proving to be no different.

It was windy, the seas were washing over the deck, and the sail was in the water with her sheets knotted up in the stanchions. After taking a cold, salty bath for about thirty minutes, I was able to gather and knot up most of the genoa on the deck, but I was unable to untangle her sheets enough to pull it completely in. The genoa hung partially in the water, along the starboard side stanchions, in some ungodly twisted knot, but it was grounded enough that I felt I could proceed without it affecting navigation. I then turned my efforts to reefing the mainsail.

This sail only had one reef point, although most have two or three, leaving me with limited ability to reef her main, but I released the mainsail halyard and let the sail down to the reef point. Then I cleated the halyard line and tied in the reefing tacks along the boom. This left me with the genoa down and a reefed mainsail.

As I gathered myself, I worked my way back to the tiller. As I did, I paused for a moment and took a good look around. I then realized that I was the only fool on the bay. There was not another boat within view. Not an oyster boat, not a tanker, not even a duck. I was all alone out there.

I could see that my marine radio had been destroyed by the water intrusion, and my cell phone had also hit the drink. I was shivering from being soaked by the cold April waters that were about 55° Fahrenheit, but I was being chilled further from the gusty winds as my saturated heavy clothing offered me no warmth or shelter from the elements. This was when I realized that I just might not be immortal. This trip just might be my last if I didn't fight to survive.

There was no hollering, "Uncle," or giving up. There was no one to rescue me or call for help. I was truly going to have to be self-sufficient and fight for my own survival, or I could potentially perish because of my own actions. This was a new reality for me, and I don't know that every man has had such an experience in his life, but it's a true awakening as to how precious life is.

I started to think about what my family would have to go through if I were to turn up missing or dead. A wash of self-pity was thrown in the mix of emotions, and a flash of all the things I had yet to accomplish.

It was time to take control and get *Genie* back into port. With the water intrusion into *Genie's* cabin, she had started to become slow to respond. Water was building up in her cabin faster than the bilge pump could vacate it. I was now east of marker 85A, out much farther than I wanted to be.

I took the tiller in hand and pushed the handle hard to the port side as I let some slack in the main sheet. This brought *Genie* to a new heading—south-southwesterly at about 200°.

The waves continued to roll over the gunwales on the starboard side and exit on the leeward side of the boat as I proceeded down the bay on a starboard tack. Yesterday's blisters were now bleeding bad, and the main sheet was stained with red and various colors of red-brown blood. My fingers were blue and gray from the bone-chilling cold and hours of clenching the tiller and sheets. I had the mainsail almost all the way out as I continued to make my way toward channel markers 83A and 81A.

I had considered taking shelter in Rockhold Creek, but there was the issue of the winds coming out of the west-northwest. I would have to set my bearing to 230° all the way back to marker 85A in order to make the channel on my starboard tack. This would have also required me to risk crossing the sandbar to round red marker #4. With the waves in the five- to seven-foot range and the troughs so deep, I knew there could not be two feet of water over the sand bar at this point. There was no way, in these high seas and high gusty winds, that I would even consider rounding red marker #2, and then tacking and heading north up the designated channel into Rockhold Creek. I figured that would take just as long and be much riskier than continuing my trip directly to Breezy Point.

Within an hour, I had sailed past Herring Bay and was approaching Holland Point. I was happy to see North Beach as I continued my journey south-southwest. There was no boardwalk, as I recall, back in the day, but I believe a fishing pier was there because I thought maybe someone would see me if I came in close enough.

As I tried to head inward, toward the shallower waters, I noticed I had started to bump into the bottom. This was not good. If I got *Genie* grounded out there, she would surely lay over on her side and sink. I was in dangerous waters and, to make it worse, the shallower the water, the greater the waves and choppier the seas became.

I headed out a little as I passed Holland Point on my starboard side and marker 81A on my port. Before long, I was passing the Rod and Reel Restaurant. I entertained the thought of slipping into the fishing creek, but I was not sure of the water depth. This would also require me to sail almost straight upwind from this point and, under the current conditions, I was sure that was not something I could do without grounding *Genie* in the restrictive channel.

I gave some thought to using the little engine, but I knew the prop was only touching the water every now and then. It was out as much as it was in the water, and I was sure it did not have the power to overcome the wind and seas that I was now facing.

Onward on a course of about 200° south-southwest, I sailed.

As I passed the town of Chesapeake Beach, the red and white radar array of the US Navy facility came into view. This was a welcome sight because I knew that not far past the tower were the cliffs of Camp Roosevelt and the cliffs of the Willows.

The wind and waves continued to pound *Genie*, and I was now hanging on in what seemed to be a cramped position as I continued to shake uncontrollably, my teeth chattering so badly that I could not make them stop. I was turning blue, and although I knew it was about 50° outside, I felt as though I was going to somehow freeze to death.

Enduring another half an hour or so, I spied green can #1, marking the channel into Breezy Point. I knew I would have to come in on the north side of the marker, leaving it on my port side as I entered the channel.

As I sailed *Genie* past Breezy Point Beach and Campground and navigated toward the entrance of the channel, I could see a few people lined up along the beach.

Within moments, I was within the confines of Plum Point Creek channel and, just as fast as it had all started, it ended. The winds had died so fast that it almost threw me to the other side of the boat as *Genie* glided down from an almost hydroplaning stance to a slow, smooth procession up the creek toward the Breezy Point Marina. Under the power lines and into the marina, she moved, making only a ripple on the surface.

As I proceeded toward her slip, I heaved a sigh of relief. I had made it. No matter what anyone else knew or said, I knew deep inside that my Maker had had a hand in guiding me safely home.

I found that I could no longer stand at will as I worked to navigate *Genie* into her designated slip. However, Mike Strandquist, the marina owner, came running over as I grabbed the first piling I came to and threw me a line. As Mike pulled *Genie* into the slip, I worked to stand and get myself on the pier.

Mike had a smile on his face that made me want to smile, as well, even though I really did not feel like I could with such a chatter going on. He took over tying up *Genie* and wanted to know if I needed him to help secure her. I told him that *Genie* would be all right for a while and that I would come back tomorrow and fix her up. I asked him to just put the padlock on the cabin hatch and everything else would be fine.

Mike leaped into action, boarding *Genie*, and dropped the mainsail. He then gathered it onto the boom and tied it with the lanyard that he'd found in the boat. Next, he worked to gather *Genie's* genoa out of the water and untangle her sheets from the stanchions. He gathered the sail and placed it in the cabin, letting me know that it would need to dry out soon or it would get moldy. Lastly, he installed the manway hatch and placed the padlock on the sliding cover to secure *Genie* for the night.

I thanked Mike as I stood there, shivering and chattering, with bloody, cold, blue and gray hands.

Mike told me that day that he had never seen anyone sail a boat like *Genie* in weather like that. He told me that the hull of *Genie* had been disappearing with each wave, and they could see the waves entering the cockpit. He told me that a whole group of folks had noticed the boat was in trouble as it had approached the Plum Point channel marker and that it had been broadcasted over the marine radio that there was a small sailboat heading south that was in jeopardy. He shared with me that all those folks out there on the beach had been there to cheer me on, in hopes that I would make it. With that, Mike suggested I should become a sailing instructor or something, but no matter what, I should get my captain's license.

He followed me to my car. Then, as I sat in the driver's seat and started it up, he signaled me to roll down the window. Mike gave me one of his smiles and told me that after I got rested up, I should sit down and take notes about the trip. He told me that an adventure like that was what books were made of. "One day, you may want to take the time to write a book about this experience." Then he said that he'd had a similar experience in his life and regretted not taking the time to write it down.

And so, in Mike's statement, there was wisdom, and this book is the result of that fleeting comment. It was not until much later in my life did I find out that Mike had been involved in a heroic boat rescue back during Hurricane Agnes, in June of 1972. I imagine the similar experience that he had referred to was most likely that event. I am sure anyone who knew Mike would have loved to have read that book.

Chapter Fourteen:
Regretful Separation

During the summer of 2002, I spent many a Saturday morning running to the marina and taking *Genie* out on short half-day cruises. I would take her on an upwind leg, tacking back and forth for about an hour or so, and then take her on a broad reach, returning to port on a fast reach of the opposite tack. Occasionally, I would get caught in dead air on the Chesapeake, as summer is known to be less than pleasant when the winds die down and the decks get extremely hot. But, for the most part, I made the round trip under sail and always returned to Breezy Point with a smile, having spent some time on the water.

On one such occasion, I was sailing back to the Plum Point Creek channel and came across two men in an aluminum Jon boat. They had been out fishing in their approximately sixteen-foot craft with some ungodly large engine on it that had apparently failed.

These men had been out, baking in the sun, for four to six hours when I happened upon them. They had obviously been drinking and had run out of beer some hours before my arrival, not thinking that the melted ice in the cooler was suitable for drinking or maybe not having their wits about them. They were burned up, dehydrated, and adrift.

As I approached these two, long-haired men, they gave me the thank-God-we-are-rescued look. I asked if they needed help, and they yelled out, "Yes," as I was passing them. So, I did a complete turn with *Genie* and circled back around for another pass.

Now, these men were most definitely not used to sailboats, for sure, because they appeared to not understand that I could not just put *Genie* in reverse and stop. I had to point her into the wind to stop her, which was no easy task in close proximity to this boat needing rescue.

I eventually got them to toss me their bow line so I could pull them in closer. As I did, these men gave me the impression of men who had been stranded on some desert island for years. They were extremely thin, and I could see their rib bones as I approached. Both had weathered, wrinkly skin, with a texture like that of a raisin. They were sporting a dark tan on their arms, but their chests and backs were bright red from sun exposure. I thought to myself that maybe they should have kept their T-shirts on, but what do I know?

I handed a few water bottles to them, which they started to drink immediately. I then told them that I would tow them into Breezy Point Marina, as we were not far from the entrance to the channel and that was my destination.

Only one of them spoke to me, and he said they wanted to go to Rockhold Creek. I explained that this was a sailboat, and with the wind coming from the north, it would take half a day just to get there. I told them that there was a bait and tackle shop just inside the creek channel where they could call someone to get help or maybe even get someone to look at the motor.

The one man who was doing all the talking told me that he did not want to be seen being towed by a sailboat and that he wanted me to release them once inside the channel so they could paddle in themselves.

I could not believe these guys. They were half-dead, adrift on the bay in light winds, with one small paddle that was from some kid's blowup raft or something, and they were starting to become quite demanding about how they were going to be rescued.

I snickered to myself and told the guy that the tide was going out, and he would never be able to paddle in with that paddle. He eventually agreed to let me take him into the marina.

As we got underway, I trimmed *Genie's* sail and headed toward the channel entrance.

As I looked back at this motley crew of raisins on the end of this tow line, it occurred to me that I needed to photograph this to document the story, as this story was totally unbelievable. So, I pulled out my camera, pointed it at the boat and its crew, and snapped a shot.

That was it. It was all these men could take. They started cursing and yelling at me as I fired off a few more photographs. They were now threatening to kill me, and all kinds of profanities were spewing out of their mouths.

The one man started to pull on the tow rope and bring himself within reach of *Genie* and myself with a large knife drawn. So, with only a moment's hesitation, I released them, setting them adrift once again as they yelled and screamed at me. I knew that it would be best if I got *Genie* docked as quickly as possible and made an exit from the marina before the raisin gang could get into port.

As I tied *Genie's* dock lines, I put a call out on the marine radio, announcing that there were two men stranded in a small aluminum boat near the channel entrance. Then I locked *Genie* up and left the marina. I don't know if anyone ever came to their rescue, but I did not lose any sleep over cutting them loose. I only wish I could locate the photos that I took that day and share them with you, but they seem to have been lost to time.

After my summer of fun and sailing runs, it became obvious once again that *Genie's* lack of freeboard was going to limit my ability to sail during the fall and spring. She was great for sailing in fair weather, with light winds and less than one-foot seas. She had proven she could handle much more, but there was no pleasure in pushing her beyond her limitations. She was just not built for anything above 10 knot winds and seas greater than a foot and a half. I swore I would never subject her or myself to anything above that again.

All good things must come to an end, and this was the case for *Genie* and myself. When fall came, I had her pulled and put on the hard as I watched other sailboats go out for a splash. All that winter, I started thinking about finding a boat with a little more freeboard and a boat that would sail faster.

Eventually, I stumbled on a twenty-seven-foot Cal boat that could sail fast and in much heavier weather than *Genie*. So, I put my beloved *Genie* up for sale on the internet. Within hours, she was sold and, at that moment, I was happy. I had enough cash in my hand to purchase the Cal and make the necessary repairs. I made all the arrangements to transfer *Genie* by mail, and I never even visited the marina to see her go.

Genie at Breezy Point Store, November 2002, on her last voyage with me. She is heading out of Plum Point Channel just before the power lines.

As I worked on the Cal that following summer, I started to regret having let *Genie* go. Sure, the Cal was a bit larger and had plenty of free board, she sailed faster and took the heavy seas with a bit more grace, but she did not have the same classic lines that I had become familiar with. The Cal was built differently, and I just never felt the same way about her as I had about *Genie*, the little 23' South Coast of the Chesapeake.

Eventually, I sold the Cal, too. To this day, though, I only regret having let my *Genie* go. *Genie's* departure from my life is one of those rare cases where the sale of a boat was not truly a happy one. I tell myself that she went to a good home and that she is being loved. I picture her sailing the Chesapeake, and it is with great hope that the 1962, South Coast, hull number 7565 is still out there, making some captain happy.

It saddens me to think that she may be back in some boneyard, waiting for her destruction. Maybe, just maybe, with any luck, I will catch a glimpse of her once more, afloat with her sails full.

In the end, I studied and obtained my OUPV Captain six pack license, as Mike had recommended. I obtained the tow endorsement and used the license to work as a towboat operator that gave me some of the most memorable times I have ever spent on the Chesapeake. But that is a different story that I will save for another day.

The End.

Genie of the Chesapeake

Facebook Page